PADI
OPEN WATER DIVER
UNOFFICIAL GUIDE

DIVE INTO ADVENTURE.

First published in 2024.
OCEANOMADS EDITORIALS.
ISBN 9798325787041

Table of Contents:

Foreword   4

Chapter 1: **Introduction to the PADI Open Water Certification**   6
- What is PADI?
- Why Become a PADI Open Water Diver?
- Prerequisites and Requirements

Chapter 2: **The Basics of Scuba Diving**   11
- Understanding Scuba Diving
- Safety Precautions and Concerns
- Equalisation

Chapter 3: **Finding the Right Dive Center**   19
- Researching Dive Centers
- Instructor Qualifications
- Course Structure and Schedule

Chapter 4: **Enrolling in the Course**   24
- Registration Process
- Course Fees and Inclusions
- Materials and Resources

Chapter 5: **Theoretical Training**   28
- Dive Theory: Physics and Physiology
- Dive Tables and Dive Computers
- Equipment Essentials

Chapter 6: **Confined Water Training**   41
- Mastering Basic Scuba Skills
- Skill Development and Practice
- Buoyancy Control and Underwater Mobility

Chapter 7: Open Water Dives 49
- Transitioning to Open Water
- Planning and Executing Dives
- Demonstrating Skills in Real Dive Scenarios

Chapter 8: Overcoming Challenges 56
- Understanding Diving Challenges
- Dealing with Underwater Pressure
- Responding to Equipment Malfunctions

Chapter 9: Safety and Emergency Procedures 66
- First Aid for Divers
- Communication and Buddy System
- Dive Health and Fitness

Chapter 10: Final Assessments and Certification 72
- Written Exams and Practical Assessments
- Reviewing Your Performance
- Receiving Your PADI Open Water Certification

Chapter 11: Continuing Your Dive Journey 76
- Advanced Training and Specialties
- Joining the Dive Community
- Exploring Diving Destinations

Chapter 12: Tips for Responsible Diving 82
- Marine Conservation and Respect for Nature
- Minimizing Your Ecological Footprint
- Being a Conscious Diver

Logbooks: Personal Diving Logbook 86

Foreword.

Welcome to the fascinating world of **scuba diving**, a realm where terrestrial boundaries dissolve and aquatic wonders await those who **dare to explore**.

In the pages of "***DIVE INTO ADVENTURE***: The Unofficial Guide to Becoming a PADI Open Water Diver" you are about to embark on a **transformative journey** into the depths of the oceans - where mystery, beauty, and awe converge.

As someone who has always been captivated by the allure of **the underwater world**, I understand the excitement and anticipation that come with taking those first steps into the blue abyss.

As an experienced **Divemaster**, I also recognise the importance of knowledge, preparation, and safety required in this **exhilarating pursuit**.

This book was written to be your **trusty companion**, a beacon of guidance that illuminates the path from curious novice to certified diver.

Whether you're standing on the verge of your very first dive or you're eager to expand your **underwater horizons**, the chapters within these pages will serve as your roadmap, your mentor, and your inspiration.

From the **fundamentals of scuba diving** to finding the right dive centre, mastering essential skills, and **earning your PADI Open Water Certification**, this book provides a comprehensive and accessible resource for all.

As you navigate these chapters, remember that diving is not just about donning equipment and descending into the deep; it's about **forging a connection** with the aquatic world, gaining an understanding of its **delicate ecosystems**, and becoming a **steward of its preservation**.

Beyond the certification, scuba diving has the power to **change your life.** It's a journey of **self-discovery**, a testament to human curiosity and courage, and a reminder of the immense beauty and **fragility of our oceans**.

So, as you turn the pages and absorb the wisdom contained within, do so with enthusiasm and an open heart. Know that **responsible diving is at the heart of this endeavour**, and this book encourages you to embrace this ethos as you venture beneath the waves.

Dive into Adventure, savour the mysteries of the deep, and, most importantly, cherish the privilege of exploring the depths of our planet's last frontier - **the oceans**.

May this book be your guiding light on this remarkable journey. With fins and masks at the ready, let the adventure begin!

Safe and exhilarating diving,

Capt. Giacomo Grande
PADI DIVEMASTER

Disclaimer. This book is by NO means intended to replace traditional learning tools, but rather to guide you alongside them.

CHAPTER 1:

Introduction to the PADI Open Water Certification

In order to begin your new adventure, let's start off by introducing you to the world of scuba diving - and what the **PADI Open Water Diver (OWD)** certification requires.

But before anything, you surely must of wondered... What does PADI stand for? And why is this certification so highly regarded across the globe?

Let's begin by understanding the basics.

What is PADI?

PADI stands for the "**Professional Association of Diving Instructors**."

It is a **globally recognised** organisation that specialises in scuba diving **training** and **certification**, offering a wide range of scuba diving courses, from beginner levels to advanced and specialty courses.

These courses are designed to teach individuals how to **safely** and **responsibly** explore the underwater world. Composed of both **theoretical knowledge** and **practical training,** we learn skills like underwater navigation, buoyancy control, and emergency procedures.

PADI certifications are **highly regarded** and respected in the diving community and are recognised at dive shops and destinations around the world.

Whether you're a novice looking to experience your first dive or an experienced diver seeking to expand your skills, PADI offers a structured and widely-recognised pathway to becoming a **certified scuba diver**.

Why Become an Open Water Diver?

Obtaining the PADI Open Water Diver Certification offers a multitude of **benefits** and **opportunities** for individuals interested in scuba diving.

Here are some reasons why you might consider getting certified:

- **Exploration**: With the OWD Certification, you gain access to a whole new world beneath the water's surface. You can explore vibrant coral reefs, encounter diverse marine life, and visit unique underwater environments that are not accessible to non-certified divers.

- **Travel**: Many of the world's most beautiful and renowned dive destinations require divers to hold a certification. Having your PADI OWD Certification opens up opportunities to dive in exotic locations and experience some of the planet's most breathtaking underwater scenery.

- **Community**: Scuba diving is a social activity, and becoming certified allows you to join a global community of divers. You'll meet like-minded individuals who share your passion for the underwater world, and you can participate in group dives and dive-related events.

- **Adventure**: Diving offers a sense of adventure and exploration. Whether you're exploring a sunken shipwreck, swimming alongside majestic sea creatures, or discovering underwater caves, each dive is a unique and thrilling adventure.

- **Personal Growth**: Scuba diving challenges you both mentally and physically. Obtaining your certification is not only an achievement but also an opportunity for personal growth. You'll gain confidence, improve your problem-solving skills, and learn to adapt to different environments.

- **Career Opportunities**: If you're passionate about diving, your PADI OWD Certification can be the first step toward a career in the dive industry. PADI offers instructor-level certifications that can open doors to teaching diving professionally.

- **Environmental Awareness**: PADI courses often include environmental education, fostering a sense of responsibility and care for marine ecosystems. As a certified diver, you can become an advocate for marine conservation and promote responsible diving practices worldwide.

- **Safety**: Safety is paramount in scuba diving, and the PADI OWD Certification ensures you receive thorough training in essential skills and safety protocols. This knowledge and training help you dive safely and confidently, reducing the risk of accidents or injuries.

- **Attributes:** With a PADI Open Water Diver certification, you can dive anywhere in the world up to 18m/60ft, book dive excursions with boats or resorts, get air fills and rent scuba tanks, rent scuba gear, and meet fellow ocean lovers from the world's largest diver community.

Prerequisites and Requirements:

1. Minimum Age: You must be at least 10 years old to enroll in the PADI OWD course. However, for divers under the age of 15, there are some restrictions on the depth of dives and the supervision required.

2. Medical Fitness: You should be in good general health to participate in scuba diving. PADI requires you to complete a medical questionnaire. Depending on your case, you may need to obtain a physician's clearance before starting the course.

3. Swimming Skills: You'll need to demonstrate water competency, including the ability to swim 200 metres/yards with no aids or 300 metres/yards with mask, fins and snorkel, and you must be able to tread water or float for 10 minutes.

4. Course Materials: You'll need the PADI OWD manual or the digital version (eLearning), which contains the foundational knowledge required for the course. You may also need access to a dive computer, which is often included during your course duration.

6. Time Commitment: The PADI OWD course typically includes both classroom or eLearning sessions and in-water training. Be prepared to spend a few days completing these components, although you can become a certified diver in as little as four days. The exact schedule may vary depending on the dive center's program.

7. Course Fee: There is a course fee associated with the PADI OWD course. This fee covers your training, certification materials, and often includes the use of scuba equipment during the course. Prices can vary depending on the location and the dive centre you choose.

8. Equipment: While dive centres often provide basic scuba equipment for training purposes, you may be required to have some personal gear, such as a mask and snorkel. Some divers also prefer to purchase their own wetsuit, booties and fins for comfort and hygiene reasons.

CHAPTER 2:

The Basics of Scuba Diving

Scuba diving is an **exhilarating** activity that allows you to **explore** the **underwater world** and all its marvels.

However, before you jump into the deep end, it's crucial to understand the basics of scuba diving to ensure your **safety** and **enjoyment**.

In this chapter, we'll cover the **fundamental** aspects of scuba diving.

Understanding Scuba Diving

What is Scuba Diving?

Scuba diving stands for "***Self-Contained Underwater Breathing Apparatus.***" It is a mode of underwater diving whereby divers use independent breathing equipment that is entirely non-reliant on a surface air supply.

Diving Techniques and Skills to Master

Scuba diving requires mastery of various techniques and skills to ensure a safe and enjoyable underwater experience.

Let's view the essential diving techniques and skills that every diver must master.

Breathing Underwater: Mastering the art of breathing underwater is fundamental to scuba diving. Proper breathing techniques not only ensure efficient air consumption but also contribute to relaxation and comfort underwater.

- **Regulator Breathing:** Practice breathing calmly and steadily through the regulator. Inhale slowly and deeply, allowing the regulator to deliver air smoothly. Exhale fully and steadily, ensuring a continuous flow of bubbles.

- **Air Conservation:** Conserve air by avoiding rapid or shallow breathing. Focus on breathing from the diaphragm rather than the chest, which reduces air consumption. Maintain a relaxed and calm demeanor underwater to minimize unnecessary exertion.

Buoyancy Control: Achieving neutral buoyancy is essential for effortless diving and minimizing the impact on the underwater environments and ecosystems.

- **Neutral Buoyancy Techniques:** Experiment with your buoyancy control device (BCD) to achieve neutral buoyancy at different depths. Practice adding and releasing small amounts of air to ascend and descend gradually. Use your breath to fine-tune buoyancy adjustments.

- **Trim Control:** Practice maintaining a horizontal body position (trim) by adjusting your buoyancy and weight distribution. Engage your core muscles to stabilize your body and avoid excessive tilting forward or backward. Use gentle fin kicks to maintain forward motion without disrupting buoyancy.

Equalisation: Equalization is a vital skill in scuba diving, allowing divers to equalize the pressure in their ears and sinuses as they descend underwater. Failure to equalize properly can result in discomfort or injury, such as barotrauma.

- **Understanding Equalization:** Equalization is the process of equalizing the pressure between the middle ear and the surrounding environment. As you descend underwater, the increasing water pressure compresses the air spaces in your ears and sinuses, causing discomfort if not equalized. The Eustachian tube, a narrow passage connecting the middle ear to the back of the throat, plays a crucial role in equalization. By opening the Eustachian tube, you allow air to flow into the middle ear, equalizing pressure.

Keep reading to learn all about Equalisation in the following chapters.

Communication: Clear communication is vital for maintaining safety and coordination among dive buddies.

- **Hand Signals:** Learn and practice a standardized set of hand signals for essential messages such as OK, out of air, how much air you have left, and navigation signs. Use clear and deliberate hand signals, ensuring they are easily understood by your dive buddy.

- **Buddy System:** Establish clear communication protocols with your dive buddy before the dive. Maintain visual contact and proximity with your buddy throughout the dive, using touch signals if visibility is limited. Establish regular communication checks to ensure both divers are aware of each other's status.

Navigation: Effective navigation skills are crucial for exploring dive sites and safely returning to the surface. Familirize yourself with compass use and mapping to prevent getting lost.

- **Compass Use:** Practice taking compass bearings on land. Underwater, hold the compass level and steady, aligning it with known landmarks or reference points. Follow compass headings accurately, adjusting for current drift if necessary.

- **Underwater Mapping:** Sketch a simple map of the dive site, noting key features, entry and exit points, and prominent landmarks. Practice underwater orientation by correlating your map with actual underwater landmarks and features.

Safety Precautions and Concerns

Safety is **paramount** in scuba diving. This section delves into various safety aspects of scuba diving to ensure that divers are **well-prepared** and **knowledgeable** about potential risks and precautions.

Safety First

You should always emphasize the importance of safety in scuba diving as the top priority. Safety should always come before any other aspect of the dive.

Being aware of the potential risks and hazards associated with scuba diving can prevent serious incidents from occurring. For this reason, the need for proper training and certification is essential, and divers should never attempt to dive beyond their training and experience level.

Understanding Potential Risks

Scuba diving involves inherent risks, including but not limited to:

- **Underwater currents**: Strong currents can pose a hazard to divers, potentially causing them to drift away from the dive site or expend excess energy.

- **Marine life encounters**: While most marine life is harmless, encounters with certain species can lead to injuries.

- **Equipment malfunctions**: Malfunctions in scuba diving equipment, such as regulators or buoyancy control devices, can compromise diver safety and require prompt action.

- **Barotrauma**: Changes in pressure during ascent and descent can lead to barotrauma, causing injuries to the ears, sinuses, or lungs if not equalized properly.

Training and Certification

Proper training and certification are essential for safe scuba diving. Divers should undergo training with a reputable diving organization, such as PADI, and obtain certification at each level of training.

Certification ensures that divers have the knowledge, skills, and experience necessary to dive safely and responsibly.

Medical Considerations

Not all individuals are suitable for scuba diving due to various medical factors. Before starting any scuba diving training or diving activities, divers should undergo a medical evaluation by a physician.

The physician will assess factors such as medical history, fitness level, and pressure sensitivity to determine if diving is safe for the individual.

After obtaining medical clearance from a physician, divers can proceed with confidence, knowing that they have addressed any potential medical concerns and are physically fit to dive.

Insurance

In scuba diving, as in any adventurous pursuit, it's wise to prepare for the unexpected. Insurance plays a crucial role in providing financial protection and peace of mind for divers.

- **Dive Accident Insurance:** Dive accident insurance provides coverage for medical expenses related to diving injuries, including decompression sickness (DCS) treatment, hyperbaric chamber sessions, and emergency medical transportation.

- **Equipment Insurance:** Scuba diving equipment can be expensive to replace or repair. Equipment insurance provides coverage for loss, theft, or damage to dive gear, ensuring that divers can continue their underwater adventures without financial burden in the event of equipment-related issues.

Equalisation

Equalisation is a crucial technique in scuba diving that divers use to balance the pressure between the inside and outside of their ears and sinuses as they descend or ascend in the water.

The primary purpose of equalisation is to prevent **barotrauma**, which is the physical damage caused by pressure differences between the inside and outside of the body.

Here's how equalisation works and why it's essential in scuba diving:

Pressure Changes in Water: As you descend underwater, the pressure increases - every 33 feet (10 meters) of depth adds roughly another atmosphere (atm) of pressure.

This pressure change affects the air spaces in your body, particularly the ears and sinuses.

Ear and Sinus Barotrauma: The ear and sinus cavities are air-filled spaces. When you descend, the increasing water pressure compresses the air inside these spaces.

If the pressure isn't equalised, it can lead to barotrauma, which can cause; ear pain, ear barotrauma (damage to the ear structures), or sinus barotrauma (pain and potential injury to the sinus cavities).

Equalisation Techniques: To prevent barotrauma, divers use techniques to adjust the pressure inside their ears and sinuses to match the external water pressure. There are two primary methods for equalisation:

- Valsalva Maneuver: This is the most common equalisation technique. To perform it, you pinch your nose shut and gently blow air through your nose while keeping your mouth closed. This action increases the air pressure inside your ears and sinuses, equalising it with the external pressure.

- Frenzel Maneuver: This technique involves pinching your nose shut and using the muscles at the back of your throat to push a small amount of air into your ears. It's a more controlled method often used by experienced divers and can be more effective for deep dives.

When to Equalise: Equalisation should be performed early and often during a dive. It's essential to equalise as soon as you start descending and continue to do so every few feet or meters as you go deeper.

Similarly, you should equalise during ascent, especially during safety stops or when returning to the surface.

Listen to Your Body: Pay attention to the sensation of fullness or pressure in your ears. These sensations are signs that it's time to equalise.

It's essential not to ignore these signals or push through discomfort, as doing so can lead to injury.

Equalization Tips:

- **Start equalizing early:** Begin equalizing as soon as you start your descent, ideally before you feel discomfort.

- **Equalize frequently:** Equalize every few feet or meters of descent to prevent pressure buildup in the ears.

- **Pay attention to your body:** If you experience pain or difficulty equalizing, ascend slightly and try again until you can equalize comfortably.

- **Avoid forceful equalization:** Never force equalization, as this can also cause injury.

CHAPTER 3:

Finding the Right Dive Center

Choosing the right **dive centre** is a pivotal step on your journey toward obtaining your PADI Open Water Certification.

This chapter will serve as your guide in selecting a dive centre that aligns with your **goals** and ensures a **safe** and **enjoyable** learning experience.

Researching Dive Centers

The importance of selecting the right dive centre is crucial as it sets the **foundation** for your entire diving experience. Make sure to research online and ask around for personal recommendations.

Some important factors to keep in mind are;

Reputation and Experience:

- **Online Reviews and Recommendations:** Research dive centers online and read reviews from past customers. Look for positive feedback regarding safety standards, quality of instruction, and overall customer satisfaction.

- **Local Recommendations:** Seek recommendations from local dive clubs, forums, or experienced divers in your area. Personal referrals can provide valuable insights into the reputation and performance of dive centers.

Certification and Accreditation:

- **PADI Centers:** Verify that the dive center is affiliated with reputable diving organizations such as PADI. PADI certification ensures that instructors adhere to high standards of training and safety.

- **Accreditation and Awards:** Look for dive centers that have received industry recognition or awards for excellence in training, safety, and environmental stewardship.

Facilities and Equipment:

- **Dive Equipment:** Inspect the dive center's equipment to ensure that it is well-maintained, up-to-date, and in good working condition. Quality dive gear contributes to safety, comfort, and overall diving experience.

- **Training Facilities:** Evaluate the dive center's training facilities, including classrooms, pool or confined water areas, and equipment rental services. A well-equipped dive center provides a conducive learning environment for students and offers convenient access to necessary gear.

Environmental Conservation Efforts:

- **Ecological Awareness:** Choose dive centers that demonstrate a commitment to environmental conservation and sustainable diving practices. Look for initiatives such as reef preservation projects, marine debris clean-up efforts, and eco-friendly dive practices.

- **Environmental Education:** Opt for dive centers that incorporate environmental education and awareness into their training programs. Understanding the importance of marine ecosystems and minimizing impact on fragile habitats contributes to responsible diving practices.

Location and Dive Sites:

- **Proximity to Dive Sites:** Consider the dive center's location in relation to popular dive sites and attractions. Convenient access to a diverse range of dive sites enhances the flexibility and variety of diving opportunities.

- **Dive Site Selection:** Inquire about the dive center's selection of dive sites and the range of underwater environments available, such as reefs, wrecks, and marine reserves. A diverse selection of dive sites caters to divers of all interests and experience levels.

Instructor Qualifications

The significance of the instructor's expertise may well be the most important factor, as nothing will replace the role of a **competent and experienced instructor** in your training.

Here are key considerations to evaluate when assessing instructor qualifications;

- **Certifications and Credentials:** Verify that the instructors at the dive center hold up to date certifications from recognized diving organizations such as PADI. These certifications demonstrate that instructors have undergone rigorous training and evaluation to meet industry standards for teaching scuba diving.

- **Experience and Expertise:** Assess the experience and expertise of the instructors, including their diving background, teaching tenure, and specialization areas. Look for instructors with extensive diving experience across a variety of environments, as well as additional certifications or endorsements in specialized diving disciplines such as deep diving, underwater navigation, or rescue diving.

- **Teaching Style and Communication Skills:** Evaluate the instructors' teaching style and communication skills to ensure compatibility with your learning preferences and needs. Effective instructors should be patient, attentive, and adept at conveying complex diving concepts in a clear, engaging manner. They should also foster a supportive learning environment that encourages questions, feedback, and active participation from students.

By thoroughly assessing instructor qualifications, you can ensure that you receive high-quality instruction, personalized guidance, and a safe learning environment throughout your scuba diving journey.

Course Structure and Schedule

The course structure and schedule offered by a dive center play a significant role in shaping the learning experience and convenience for students.

When evaluating course structure and schedule look for;

- **Training Facilities:** Ensure that the facilities are well-maintained, adequately equipped, and conducive to effective learning. Access to modern teaching aids, such as multimedia presentations, instructional videos, and interactive simulations, can enhance the learning experience and facilitate skill development.

- **Instructor-to-Student Ratio:** Inquire about the instructor-to-student ratio maintained by the dive center during training sessions. Smaller class sizes and personalized instruction allow for more individualized attention, feedback, and support from instructors.

- **Flexibility and Availability:** Consider the flexibility and availability of course scheduling options offered by the dive center. Choose a dive center that offers a range of course dates, times, and formats to accommodate your schedule and learning preferences.

- **Course Duration and Progression:** Evaluate the duration and progression of the course to determine the time commitment required and the pace of learning.

- **Additional Training Opportunities:** Inquire about any additional training opportunities or enrichment programs offered by the dive center, such as specialty courses, workshops, or guided dive excursions. These opportunities allow you to further expand your diving skills, knowledge, and experience beyond the basic certification level, enhancing your proficiency and enjoyment as a diver.

CHAPTER 4:

Enrolling in the Course

Once you have decided where you will be doing your PADI Open Water Diver course you can proceed to enrol and **start your training**.

Each dive centre will talk you through the specific steps required to get you learning as soon as possible.

Here are a few things to consider when doing so;

Registration Process

- **Contacting the Dive Center:** Reach out to the dive center of your choice to inquire about course availability and registration procedures. You can usually do this by phone, email, or visiting the dive center in person. Be prepared to provide basic personal information and specify your preferred course dates and certification level.

- **Completing Enrollment Forms:** Upon selecting a course and confirming availability, you will be required to complete enrollment forms provided by the dive center. These forms typically include liability waivers, medical questionnaires, and terms of agreement. Ensure that you provide accurate and truthful information to facilitate a smooth enrollment process.

- **Submitting Payment:** Depending on the dive center's policies, you may be required to submit a deposit or full payment at the time of registration to secure your spot in the course. Payment methods may include credit card, bank transfer, or cash. Review the dive center's payment terms and cancellation policies before making any payments.

Course Fees and Inclusions

- **Understanding Course Fees:** Dive course fees vary depending on factors such as certification level, course duration, and location. Inquire about the total cost of the course, including any additional fees for equipment rental, certification processing, or course materials. Request a detailed breakdown of fees to ensure transparency and avoid unexpected expenses.

- **Inclusions and Exclusions:** Clarify what is included in the course fees, such as instructional materials, equipment rental, certification fees, and dive site access. Some dive centers may offer package deals that include accommodation, meals, or additional training opportunities. Be aware of any items or services that are not included in the course fees and budget accordingly.

Materials and Resources

- **Course Materials:** Dive courses typically require students to study course materials such as textbooks, manuals, and multimedia resources to prepare for classroom sessions and practical training. Inquire about the recommended course materials and where to obtain them. Some dive centers provide course materials as part of the course fees, while others may require students to purchase them separately.

- **Online Learning Platforms:** Many dive organizations offer online learning platforms or e-learning modules that allow students to complete the theoretical portion of the course remotely before attending in-person sessions. Check if your chosen dive center offers online learning options and how to access them.

- **Additional Resources:** In addition to course materials, consider investing in supplementary resources such as diving reference books, dive planning tools, and dive computer manuals to enhance your understanding of diving principles and techniques. These resources can serve as valuable references throughout your diving education and beyond.

CHAPTER 5:
Theoretical Training

Welcome to the classroom portion of your **PADI Open Water** course.

In this chapter, we'll dive into the **essential knowledge** development phase, where you'll gain a deep understanding of **dive theory**, **safety protocols**, and the **principles of scuba diving.**

This foundational knowledge is a crucial step in becoming a **confident** and **responsible** diver.

Dive Theory: Physics and Physiology

Theoretical Foundations of Diving

Before strapping on your gear and descending into the depths, it's crucial to understand the theoretical underpinnings of scuba diving.

Scuba diving is more than just a physical activity—it's a fascinating blend of **science**, **technology**, and **exploration**.

Dive Physics

Dive physics is a branch of science that explores the **physical principles governing the behaviour of matter and energy underwater.**

As a scuba diver, understanding dive physics is crucial because it influences your safety, buoyancy control, decompression planning, and overall dive experience.

Let's delve into the key concepts of dive physics.

Pressure and Depth:

- **Pressure**: Underwater, pressure increases with depth. Every **33 feet** (**10 meters**) you descend, you experience an additional atmosphere (atm) of pressure. The pressure is exerted uniformly in all directions, affecting your body, the air in your cylinder and the rest of your equipment.

- **Boyle's Law**: This law states that as pressure increases, the volume of a gas decreases, and vice versa. It's relevant to scuba diving because it explains how the air in your tank compresses as you descend and expands as you ascend.

Buoyancy:

- **Archimedes' Principle:** This principle explains buoyancy and why objects float or sink in fluids. An object immersed in a fluid experiences an upward buoyant force equal to the weight of the fluid it displaces. Divers use this principle to control their buoyancy with the help of their buoyancy control devices (BCDs).

Gases in Diving:

- **Dalton's Law:** Dalton's law states that in a mixture of gases, each gas exerts pressure independently as if it occupied the entire space. In scuba diving, this law is essential for understanding how the partial pressures of oxygen and nitrogen in the breathing gas affect your body.

- **Henry's Law:** Henry's law explains how gases dissolve in liquids at varying pressures. As you descend while diving, the higher pressure causes more nitrogen and other gases to dissolve in your body tissues. Ascending releases these gases, which can lead to decompression sickness if not managed properly.

Air and Nitrox in Scuba Diving:

In scuba diving, the breathing gases divers use play a crucial role in their safety and dive duration. Two common gases used in scuba diving are air and nitrox. Let's explore each of these gases in detail:

1. Air:

- **Composition:** The air we breathe on the surface is primarily composed of approximately **21% oxygen** and **79% nitrogen**, with trace amounts of other gases like carbon dioxide and argon. In scuba diving, the term "air" refers to a compressed and filtered version of this atmospheric air.

- **Use in Diving:** Air is the most commonly used breathing gas in recreational scuba diving. Divers need to monitor their bottom time and depth to avoid exceeding safe limits for nitrogen absorption.

- **Benefits**: Air is readily available, and most dive shops provide it. It's suitable for recreational diving to moderate depths (typically up to **40 meters** or **130 feet**). Diving with air is cost-effective and doesn't require special training beyond Open Water certification.

- **Considerations**: Divers using air must adhere to no-decompression limits (NDLs) to avoid the risk of decompression sickness (DCS). As you go deeper or extend your dive time, your body accumulates more nitrogen, increasing the risk of DCS if you ascend too quickly.

2. Nitrox (Enriched Air Nitrox or EANx):

- **Composition**: Nitrox is a breathing gas that contains a higher percentage of oxygen (typically between **22%** and **40%**) and a reduced percentage of nitrogen compared to regular air. The most common nitrox mixtures are **EAN32** (32% oxygen) and **EAN36** (36% oxygen).

- **Use in Diving**: Nitrox is used in scuba diving to extend bottom times and reduce the risk of decompression sickness. Divers can stay underwater longer at specific depths because the reduced nitrogen content decreases nitrogen absorption. Nitrox requires special tanks, and divers must analyze the gas mixture before use.

- **Benefits**: The main advantage of nitrox is its ability to increase dive times within no-decompression limits, especially for repetitive dives. It reduces fatigue and allows for shorter surface intervals between dives. Nitrox is commonly used for dive vacations, liveaboards, and repetitive dives.

- **Considerations**: Divers using nitrox must be trained and certified in its use, typically through the PADI Enriched Air Diver course. They need to analyze the tank's gas mixture accurately and plan their dives accordingly. Diving with a high-oxygen mixture at depth carries its own set of risks, such as oxygen toxicity, which must be managed carefully.

Decompression Theory:

- **Decompression Sickness (DCS)**: This condition occurs when nitrogen bubbles form in your body tissues due to rapid ascent or exceeding no-decompression limits. Understanding the principles of decompression theory is vital for planning safe ascents and avoiding DCS.

- **Safe Ascent Profiles**: Dive tables and dive computers help divers calculate safe ascent profiles by managing nitrogen absorption and off-gassing.

Light and Colour Absorption:

- **Colour Absorption**: Water absorbs light differently than air. In the underwater world, colours appear differently and are absorbed at varying depths, filtering out certain colours. Reds, oranges, and yellows are among the first colours to vanish, leaving behind the blue and green hues. Consequently, underwater scenery often appears predominantly blue and green.

- **Underwater Magnification**: Glass has almost the same optical properties as water and very little refraction occurs as light passes from water into the mask lens. However, the density of the mask lens is much greater than the density of the air inside the mask. As light passes from the mask lens into the air it diverges (the opposite of focusing). This results in objects appearing larger than they would out of the water. The magnification is about **25%** so that a 16-inch (40cm) long fish will appear to be 20 inches (50cm) in length.

Sound Underwater:

- **Speed of Sound**: Sound travels faster underwater than in air. This can affect communication between divers, making hand signals and non-verbal communication crucial.

Dive Physiology

Let's explore the physiological aspects of diving, including how pressure affects the body, the role of breathing, and the risks associated with ascending and descending.

Decompression Theory:

Decompression theory is a fundamental concept in scuba diving that revolves around managing the safe ascent of a diver who has been exposed to increased pressure underwater.

The primary goal of decompression theory is to prevent decompression sickness (DCS), also known as "**the bends**".

The Underlying Principle: Decompression theory is based on Henry's Law, which states that the amount of gas that dissolves in a liquid is directly proportional to the partial pressure of that gas above the liquid.

In the context of diving, it means that as you descend, the increased pressure causes more nitrogen (and other gases in the breathing mix) to dissolve in your body tissues.

Nitrogen Uptake and Off-Gassing:

- Uptake: As you descend during a dive, your body absorbs nitrogen from the breathing gas mixture. This occurs because the partial pressure of nitrogen in the breathing gas increases with depth.

- Off-Gassing: When you ascend, the pressure decreases, and the excess nitrogen in your body begins to come out of solution and form gas bubbles. These bubbles can cause harm if they form too rapidly or if you ascend too quickly.

Decompression Sickness (DCS):

- **Formation of Bubbles**: DCS occurs when nitrogen bubbles form in body tissues and bloodstream due to rapid ascent or exceeding no-decompression limits (the maximum time and depth limits for a dive without requiring decompression stops).

- **Symptoms**: DCS symptoms can range from mild joint pain and rashes to severe neurological and cardiovascular symptoms. DCS can be life-threatening if not treated promptly.

In the event of suspected DCS, prompt treatment is essential.

Here's how to avoid and respond to DCS:

Prevention:

- **Plan and Monitor Dive Profiles**: Always plan your dives according to established dive tables or dive computer recommendations. These guidelines provide no-decompression limits (NDLs) based on your depth and time underwater.

- **Stay Within Your Training and Certification Limits**: Dive within the limits of your training and certification. Advanced or technical dives require specialised training to manage the increased risk of DCS.

- **Ascend Slowly**: Ascend at a controlled rate of about **9-10 meters** (**30-33 feet**) per minute. Avoid rapid ascents, which can increase the risk of DCS.

- **Safety Stops**: Conduct safety stops, typically at **3 to 5 meters** (**10 to 15 feet**) for **3 to 5 minutes**, as an extra precaution, especially after deep or extended dives.

- **Avoid Flying After Diving**: Wait at least **12 to 24 hours** after a single no-decompression dive before flying. For multiple dives or deeper dives, wait longer to allow time for off-gassing.

Recognising Symptoms:

- **Mild DCS Symptoms:** Symptoms can range from joint pain and fatigue to skin rashes. Be attentive to any unusual sensations, particularly joint pain.

- **Severe DCS Symptoms:** Severe DCS may involve neurological symptoms, such as numbness, weakness, dizziness, confusion, or loss of consciousness. These require immediate medical attention.

Treating DCS:

- **Emergency Response:** If you or a fellow diver show signs of DCS, seek emergency medical assistance immediately. Administer 100% oxygen to the affected diver if available and trained to do so.

- **Recompression Chamber:** Transport the affected diver to a hyperbaric recompression chamber as soon as possible. These chambers are the most effective treatment for DCS.

- **Stay Hydrated:** Keep the affected person well-hydrated, as this can help the body eliminate excess nitrogen more effectively.

- **Follow Medical Advice:** DCS treatment can involve multiple sessions in a hyperbaric chamber. Follow the recommendations of medical professionals for a complete recovery.

- **Preventive Measures:** After experiencing DCS, divers may be at increased risk in the future. Consult with a dive medicine specialist to assess your future diving possibilities and any additional precautions needed.

Dive Tables and Dive Computers

Decompression Tables and Dive Computers:

- **Decompression Tables:** Historically, divers used printed dive tables to plan their dives and calculate the required decompression stops. These tables are based on mathematical models that predict how nitrogen is absorbed and off-gassed during a dive.

- **Dive Computers:** Modern dive computers use algorithms to continuously calculate and update a diver's nitrogen exposure during a dive. They provide real-time information on ascent rates, no-decompression limits, and decompression stops, making dive planning more accurate and user-friendly.

Decompression Stops:

- **Safety Stops:** Many dives conclude with a safety stop at a shallower depth, typically around **15 feet** (**5 meters**), to allow for additional off-gassing and reduce the risk of DCS.

- **Decompression Stops:** For dives that exceed no-decompression limits, divers may need to make one or more mandatory decompression stops at specified depths and durations to safely off-gas excess nitrogen.

Risk Mitigation:

- **Ascent Rate:** Controlling your ascent rate is critical in managing the risk of DCS. Slower ascents allow your body more time to off-gas safely.

- **Conservative Profiles:** Many divers choose to follow conservative dive profiles that reduce their risk of exceeding no-decompression limits and requiring decompression stops.

Hyperbaric Oxygen Therapy (HBO):

- **Treatment for DCS:** In the unfortunate event of DCS, hyperbaric oxygen therapy is often used to treat the condition. It involves breathing 100% oxygen in a hyperbaric chamber to accelerate the elimination of nitrogen bubbles from the body.

Dive Planning:

- **Dive Planning Process:** Understand the steps involved in planning a dive, from selecting a dive site to calculating bottom time and ascent profiles.

- **Safety Checks:** Learn about pre-dive safety checks, like the buddy check and the five-point descent/ascent check.

- **Emergency Procedures:** Familiarise yourself with common emergency procedures, such as sharing air with your buddy and performing controlled emergency ascents.

Equipment Essentials

Scuba diving requires a specialised set of equipment to ensure your comfort, safety, and enjoyment while exploring the underwater world.

In this overview, we'll introduce you to the key pieces of scuba equipment that divers commonly use:

1. **Mask**:

- **Purpose**: A mask creates an air space in front of your eyes, allowing you to see clearly underwater. It also keeps water out of your nose.

- **Features**: Masks come in various styles, including single-lens, dual-lens, and full-face masks. They should fit comfortably, provide a watertight seal, and have tempered glass lenses for durability.

2. **Snorkel**:

- **Purpose**: A snorkel enables you to breathe at the surface while keeping your face submerged. It conserves air in your tank when you're not diving.

- **Features**: Snorkels typically have a mouthpiece, a flexible tube, and a purge valve for easy clearing. They vary in design, including simple J-tubes and more complex dry snorkels.

3. **Fins**:

- **Purpose**: Fins enhance your swimming efficiency and manoeuvrability underwater. They help conserve energy and reduce fatigue.

- **Features**: Fins come in various styles, including open-heel (worn with booties) and full-foot (worn barefoot or with thin socks). Consider the type of diving and water conditions when selecting fins.

4. **Exposure Protection**:

- **Purpose**: Exposure protection includes wetsuits and drysuits. They help regulate your body temperature by trapping a thin layer of water between your skin and the suit, which your body then warms.

- **Features**: Wetsuits are made of neoprene and come in different thicknesses for different water temperatures. Drysuits are watertight and provide insulation through air or a special lining.

5. **BCD (Buoyancy Control Device)**:

- **Purpose**: A BCD allows you to control your buoyancy by adding or releasing air from an integrated tank or a separate inflator hose.

- **Features**: BCDs have pockets for weights, D-rings for attaching gear, and an inflator/deflator mechanism. They come in jacket-style or wing-style designs.

6. **Regulator**:

- **Purpose**: A regulator is your life support system, delivering air from the tank to your mouth. It reduces the high-pressure air in the tank to a breathable pressure.

- **Components**: A regulator typically includes a first stage (connected to the tank), a second stage (your mouthpiece), a hose for each stage, and an alternate air source (octopus) for sharing air with a buddy.

7. **Dive Computer**:

- **Purpose**: A dive computer monitors your depth, dive time, and nitrogen absorption in real time. It calculates your no-decompression limits and provides vital safety information.

- **Features**: Dive computers come in wrist or console-mounted styles and can be air-integrated (showing tank pressure) or non-air-integrated.

8. **Cylinder (Tank):**

- **Purpose**: The cylinder holds compressed air or mixed gases for breathing underwater.

- **Features**: Tanks come in various materials (aluminium or steel) and sizes (measured in cubic feet or litres). Their capacity determines your available dive time.

9. **Weight System:**

- **Purpose**: Weight systems help you achieve neutral buoyancy by offsetting your natural buoyancy. You can add or ditch weights as needed.

- **Types**: Weight systems include weight belts with quick-release buckles and integrated weight pockets on BCDs.

10. **Dive Accessories:**

- **Dive Knife**: Used for safety and utility purposes, such as cutting fishing lines or entanglements.

- **Dive Lights**: Illuminate the underwater world, especially in darker or deeper conditions.

- **Compass**: A navigational tool to maintain your direction underwater.

- **Surface Marker Buoy (SMB)**: A buoy used to signal your position to boats while at the surface.

CHAPTER 6:
Confined Water Training

In this chapter, you'll take your first steps into the underwater world in a controlled and safe environment known as **confined water**.

Confined water training is a critical phase of your PADI Open Water Certification course, as it allows you to develop **essential scuba skills**, **gain confidence underwater**, and **prepare for open water dives**.

Mastering Basic Scuba Skills

Confined water training takes place in a **controlled** setting such as a swimming pool or shallow protected water. Its primary purpose is to build **essential scuba skills** and **confidence** before moving on to open water.

This phase serves as a bridge between theoretical knowledge and open-water diving. It is essential for building your foundational scuba diving skills and gaining confidence in a safe environment.

Confined Water Exercises

1. Breathing and Equalization:

- **Proper Breathing**: Master controlled, slow, and deep breathing. Avoid rapid, shallow breaths, which can increase your air consumption and stress levels. Relax and maintain a consistent rhythm.

- **Equalization**: Learn the Valsalva maneuver or the Frenzel maneuver for equalizing pressure in your ears and sinuses as you descend. Equalization is crucial to prevent barotrauma and ear pain.

2. Buoyancy Control:

- **Weighting**: Understand how to properly weight yourself for neutral buoyancy. The goal is to be able to hover effortlessly at any depth without sinking or ascending. This skill conserves energy and prevents damage to fragile aquatic life.

- **Breath Control**: Master the art of using your lungs to control your buoyancy. Inhale to rise, exhale to descend. Small adjustments in your breathing can help you maintain your desired depth.

3. Mask Skills:

- **Mask Clearing**: Practice clearing water from your mask. This skill is essential for maintaining clear vision underwater. Learn to do it calmly and efficiently.

- **Mask Removal and Replacement**: In the unlikely event of a flooded mask, know how to remove it, clear the water, and put it back on. This is a critical safety skill.

4. Regulator Skills:

- **Regulator Retrieval**: If your regulator gets knocked out of your mouth, learn how to locate and reinsert it calmly. This skill ensures you can always access your air supply.

- **Alternate Air Source**: Understand how to use your buddy's alternate air source (octopus) in case of an out-of-air emergency.

5. Finning Techniques:

- **Flutter Kick**: Master the flutter kick, a basic finning technique that provides efficient propulsion while conserving energy.

- **Frog Kick and Scissor Kick**: Explore other finning techniques like the frog kick and scissor kick, which can be more effective in different situations.

6. Underwater Communication:

- **Hand Signals**: Learn and use standard hand signals to communicate with your dive buddy underwater. Clear communication is crucial for safety and sharing the excitement of the underwater world.

7. Navigation:

- **Compass Use**: Familiarize yourself with using a dive compass to maintain your heading and navigate underwater. Basic navigation skills are vital for exploring dive sites effectively.

- **References**: Learn to take constant references such as depth readings, fixed objects and elements that stand out.

8. Safety and Emergency Procedures:

- **Buddy Checks:** Perform pre-dive safety checks (buddy checks) before each dive to ensure all equipment is in working order.

- **Emergency Ascents:** Understand how to perform controlled emergency ascents in case of out-of-air situations or other emergencies.

- **Dive Planning:** Develop good dive planning habits, including setting maximum dive times, monitoring your air supply, and staying within your dive limits.

- **Out-of-Air Situations**: Understand how to handle out-of-air emergencies by sharing air with your buddy using the alternate air source (octopus).

9. Environmental Awareness:

- **Marine Conservation**: Respect the underwater environment by avoiding contact with marine life, maintaining buoyancy control, and avoiding disturbing the seabed.

- **Dive Site Awareness**: Be aware of your surroundings and stay within the dive site boundaries. Know the entry and exit points and have a plan for surface currents.

10. Controlled Descents and Ascents:

- **Descending**: Practice controlled descents by releasing small amounts of air from your BCD.

- **Ascending**: Learn to ascend safely, maintaining proper control and a slow, controlled rate to avoid barotrauma.

Skill Development and Practice

In order to become a confident diver, practice is key. Focus on developing your skill to a point where you feel you have mastered each excercise. Just getting by the day of the exam will not cut it in the real world. If there are any skills you are not confortable with, seek assistance and practice, practice, practice!

- **Structured Learning**: Confined water training provides a structured environment for skill development, allowing divers to focus on mastering specific techniques under the guidance of a certified instructor. Each skill is introduced gradually, with ample time for practice and refinement before moving on to more advanced concepts.

- **Progressive Exercises:** Divers progress through a series of progressive exercises designed to build upon fundamental skills and increase proficiency over time. These exercises may include buoyancy drills, finning techniques, equipment handling, and emergency procedures. By starting with simple tasks and gradually increasing complexity, divers can develop confidence and competence in their abilities.

- **Repetition and Reinforcement**: Repetition is key to skill mastery, and confined water training offers ample opportunity for divers to practice skills repeatedly until they become second nature. Instructors provide constructive feedback and encouragement to help divers refine their technique and address any areas of weakness. Reinforcement through consistent practice instills muscle memory and ensures that skills are retained over time.

- **Simulated Scenarios**: Confined water training often incorporates simulated scenarios to simulate real-life diving situations and prepare divers for potential challenges. These scenarios may include simulated equipment malfunctions, buddy rescues, and emergency ascents. By practicing responses to these scenarios in a controlled environment, divers can develop confidence and readiness to handle similar situations in open water.

- **Gradual Progression**: Skill development in confined water training follows a gradual progression, with divers advancing from basic skills to more complex tasks as they gain experience and proficiency. Instructors carefully monitor divers' progress and adjust the pace of training to ensure that each individual is challenged appropriately while maintaining safety and confidence.

- **Independent Practice**: In addition to instructor-led training sessions, divers are encouraged to engage in independent practice to reinforce skills outside of structured lessons. Independent practice allows divers to develop self-reliance and confidence in their abilities, as well as to identify areas for further improvement. Dive centers may provide access to practice facilities such as pool sessions or confined water areas for divers to hone their skills between formal training sessions. Always make sure you are accompanied by a professional.

- **Continuous Learning**: Skill development is an ongoing process in scuba diving, and confined water training is just the beginning of the journey. Divers are encouraged to continue learning and refining their skills through further training, guided dives, and real-world experiences. By embracing a mindset of continuous learning and improvement, divers can expand their capabilities and enjoy a lifetime of safe and rewarding diving adventures.

Buoyancy Control and Underwater Mobility

Confined water training serves as a crucial stepping stone in your scuba diving journey, providing a controlled environment to master essential skills before venturing into open water. Focusing on two fundamental aspects of confined water training: buoyancy control and underwater mobility. By mastering these skills in a controlled setting, you'll build confidence and competence for safe and enjoyable dives in open water environments.

Buoyancy Control

- **Understanding Neutral Buoyancy**: Buoyancy control is the cornerstone of scuba diving, allowing divers to maintain their position in the water column effortlessly. Neutral buoyancy occurs when the buoyant force acting on an object equals its weight, resulting in the object neither sinking nor rising. Understanding this concept is crucial for conserving energy, maintaining depth, and maneuvering underwater with precision.

- **Buoyancy Compensator Device (BCD) Management**: The BCD is a vital piece of diving equipment that enables divers to control their buoyancy. By inflating or deflating the BCD, divers can adjust their buoyancy and ascend, descend, or maintain their position in the water column. Proper BCD management involves using quick-release mechanisms and oral inflation methods to fine-tune buoyancy during the dive, ensuring optimal control and comfort underwater.

- **Trim and Proper Weighting**: Trim refers to the diver's body position in the water, specifically the horizontal alignment of the body. Proper trim and weighting are essential for maintaining a streamlined profile and minimizing drag underwater. Experiment with different weighting configurations to achieve neutral buoyancy and proper trim, distributing weight evenly to achieve balance and stability.

Underwater Mobility:

- **Swimming Techniques**: Swimming efficiently underwater requires mastering various finning techniques. Flutter kicks, frog kicks, and modified flutter kicks are commonly used to propel divers forward with minimal effort. Proper finning techniques involve coordinating arm and leg movements to generate propulsion while minimizing energy expenditure. By practicing swimming techniques, you can move through the water with ease and precision, conserving energy and maximizing bottom time during dives.

- **Hovering and Stationary Positioning**: Hovering in place without exerting unnecessary effort is a valuable skill for divers, allowing them to observe marine life and explore their surroundings without disturbing the environment. Proper buoyancy control and breathing techniques are essential for achieving a stable, stationary position underwater. Learn to control your buoyancy by adjusting their breathing and BCD inflation, maintaining a consistent depth and position in the water column. By mastering hovering, divers can conserve energy and maintain situational awareness during dives.

- **Underwater Navigation**: Navigating underwater requires proficiency in compass navigation and natural navigation cues. Learn how to use a compass to maintain your course and navigate to predetermined waypoints underwater. Additionally, they rely on natural navigation cues such as bottom contours, landmarks, and underwater features to orient themselves and navigate effectively. Developing strong navigation skills allows divers to explore dive sites confidently and safely, enhancing their independence and enjoyment underwater.

CHAPTER 7:
Open Water Dives

Welcome to the **thrilling** climax of your scuba diving journey: the open water dives and the culmination of your efforts in obtaining the PADI Open Water Certification.

In this chapter, we'll embark on a **deep dive** into what you can expect during your open-water training and the path to becoming a **certified diver**.

Transitioning to Open Water

Open Water Dive Sessions

Open-water diving offers a **profound sense of adventure** and **connection to the natural world**. Divers are drawn to the excitement of **exploring uncharted territory**, witnessing the beauty of marine life in its natural habitat, and encountering unexpected events.

The challenges posed by open water, such as **adapting to changing conditions** and developing advanced skills, contribute to a sense of **accomplishment** and **empowerment**. It fosters a deep **respect** for the oceans and an **awareness** of the importance of responsible diving practices to preserve these incredible environments.

It's where the true adventure begins - a realm of **exploration**, **wonder**, and a lifelong journey of **discovering the mysteries** of the deep blue.

Preparing for Open Water Dives

- **Pre-Dive Safety Checks:** These are of great importance; conducting a buddy check, including equipment inspection, ensuring proper tank attachment, verifying air supply, and checking for any potential issues with each other's gear, can prevent equipment failures and unexpected surprises.

- **Dive Planning:** Choosing an appropriate dive site, considering current conditions and visibility, and setting clear dive objectives must be taken into serious consideration. Calculating no-decompression limits (NDL) based on dive tables or dive computers will ensure you remain safe at all times.

- **Emergency Procedures:** Always be prepared for common underwater emergencies, such as running low on air, equipment malfunctions, or buddy separation. Maintain proper communication with your buddy, ascend slowly to safety, and remain calm under pressure.

Exploring the Underwater World

Open water encompasses the vast, unconfined expanses of natural aquatic environments, including oceans, seas, lakes, and rivers, where divers explore the underwater world.

Characteristics

- **Varied Depths:** Open water environments can range from shallow coastal areas to deep oceanic trenches, offering diverse dive profiles.

- **Dynamic Conditions:** Divers encounter a wide array of conditions, including currents, waves, tides, and varying visibility. These conditions challenge and excite experienced divers.

- **Marine Life:** Open water exposes divers to a rich tapestry of marine life, from colourful coral reefs to majestic pelagic creatures.

- **Breathtaking Landscapes:** Stunning underwater landscapes, such as coral formations and underwater caves, captivate divers with their beauty and geological features.

- **Ethereal Lighting Effects:** Light plays a transformative role underwater, creating mesmerizing lighting effects that enhance the visual appeal of dive sites and underwater scenery.

- **Sense of Adventure:** Open water diving instills a sense of adventure and exploration, inviting divers to discover new dive sites, encounter marine life, and uncover hidden treasures.

Challenges

- **Real-World Factors:** Open water introduces divers to real-world factors like navigation, managing currents, dealing with changing conditions, and respecting the environment.

- **Buoyancy Control:** Achieving precise buoyancy control becomes crucial in open water to always keep control, avoid disturbing fragile ecosystems and conserve energy.

- **Unexpected Events:** Awareness is at the forefront of safe diving. Being aware of your surroundings and yourself, and keeping close contact with your buddies at all times is crucial to ensure everyone returns safely to the surface.

- **Underwater Navigation:** Navigating in open water environments presents challenges due to the absence of traditional landmarks, requiring reliance on compass navigation and situational awareness.

- **Limited Resources:** Divers must manage finite resources such as breathing gas and thermal protection to ensure safety and well-being throughout the dive, necessitating careful planning and monitoring.

- **Environmental Impact:** Open water divers have a responsibility to minimize their impact on fragile marine ecosystems and promote conservation efforts, practicing responsible diving behaviors and conservation practices.

Planning and Executing Dives

Planning and executing open water dives require careful consideration of various factors to ensure safety, enjoyment, and success. This chapter provides guidance on how to plan and execute dives effectively.

- **Dive Site Selection:** Research potential dive sites to assess their suitability for your skill level, interests, and dive objectives. Consider factors such as depth, currents, visibility, marine life, and accessibility when choosing dive sites. Consult local dive operators, dive guides, or online resources for information and recommendations on dive site selection.

- **Dive Planning:** Develop a dive plan that outlines the dive objectives, dive profile, maximum depth, bottom time, and safety considerations. Consider factors such as ascent and descent rates, surface intervals, and emergency procedures in your dive plan. Communicate your dive plan with your dive buddy or dive team and ensure everyone understands their roles and responsibilities.

- **Equipment Preparation**: Inspect and assemble your dive equipment, ensuring that it is in good working condition and properly configured for the dive. Double-check essential equipment such as regulators, BCDs, dive computers, and safety devices to ensure they are functioning correctly. Pack necessary spares and emergency equipment, such as spare o-rings, dive lights, and signaling devices, in case of equipment failure.

- **Safety Briefing**: Conduct a thorough pre-dive safety briefing with your dive buddy or dive team before entering the water. Review dive objectives, dive plan, emergency procedures, hand signals, and communication protocols during the safety briefing. Emphasize the importance of situational awareness, buddy communication, and adherence to safety protocols throughout the dive.

Demonstrating Skills in Real Dive Scenarios

As you progress in your training and gain experience, the ability to perform these skills confidently and effectively becomes increasingly vital for safe and enjoyable dives. This chapter will cover various aspects of skill demonstration, including skill refinement, real-world application, and scenario-based training.

- **Skill Refinement**: Divers should continuously refine and hone their scuba diving skills through regular practice and training sessions.
Focus on mastering fundamental skills such as buoyancy control, finning techniques, mask clearing, and regulator recovery, as these form the foundation of safe and efficient diving. Utilize skill development exercises such as buoyancy drills, navigation challenges, and simulated emergencies to improve proficiency and confidence underwater.

- **Real-World Application**: Apply learned skills in real dive scenarios to assess their effectiveness and practicality in different underwater environments. Practice deploying surface marker buoys, performing controlled ascents and descents, and executing emergency procedures in realistic dive conditions to simulate real-world scenarios. Gain experience in managing factors such as currents, visibility changes, and marine life encounters while demonstrating essential diving skills to enhance adaptability and readiness for diverse dive conditions.

- **Scenario-Based Training**: Incorporate scenario-based training into dive courses and skill development sessions to simulate common dive emergencies and challenging situations. Create scenarios such as equipment malfunctions, out-of-air emergencies, and lost diver situations to test divers' ability to respond effectively under pressure. Encourage divers to apply problem-solving skills, communication techniques, and teamwork strategies to resolve simulated emergencies and mitigate risks in a controlled environment.

- **Feedback and Evaluation:** Provide constructive feedback and evaluation on divers' skill performance, identifying areas for improvement and highlighting strengths. Use debriefing sessions and post-dive discussions to review dive experiences, discuss challenges encountered, and reinforce learning objectives. Offer guidance and encouragement to divers as they work towards mastering essential skills and building confidence in their abilities as competent and responsible divers.

- **Continued Practice and Development:** Emphasize the importance of ongoing skill development and continued practice beyond certification courses. Encourage divers to participate in refresher courses, skill workshops, and guided dives to maintain and enhance their proficiency in essential diving skills. Foster a culture of lifelong learning and skill refinement among divers, promoting a commitment to safety, competence, and excellence in scuba diving.

By demonstrating essential scuba diving skills in real dive scenarios, divers can build confidence, improve competence, and enhance safety underwater. Through consistent practice, scenario-based training, and ongoing skill development, divers can effectively prepare themselves to navigate the challenges and rewards of the underwater world with skill and proficiency.

CHAPTER 8:
Overcoming Challenges

Scuba diving is a **rewarding** and **exhilarating** activity, but it also comes with its fair share of **challenges**.

This chapter is dedicated to helping you **understand** and **overcome** some of the common obstacles that divers may face in their underwater adventures.

Understanding Diving Challenges

Scuba diving comes with its fair share of challenges. In order to be prepared for whatever may come our way, a good diver must be familiar with how to prevent and deal with these obstacles in the safest and most efficient manner.

Importance of Pre-Dive Equipment Checks and Maintenance

- **Pre-Dive Equipment Checks**: Before you even dip a toe into the water, taking the time for thorough pre-dive equipment checks can make all the difference in ensuring a safe and enjoyable dive. By meticulously inspecting key gear components such as regulators, masks, BCD inflators, and tanks, you can identify and address any potential issues before they become problems underwater. Collaborating with your dive buddy to verify each other's gear adds an extra layer of safety and peace of mind.

- **Regular Servicing by Certified Technicians**: Just like your car needs regular maintenance to keep it running smoothly, your diving gear requires routine servicing by certified technicians. Scheduling regular service intervals for components like regulators, BCDs, and tanks helps maintain gear performance and prevents malfunctions. Keeping detailed records of equipment servicing and replacements allows you to track gear performance over time and ensure everything is in top condition for your next dive adventure.

Buoyancy Problems

- **Understanding Neutral Buoyancy:** Picture yourself effortlessly hovering in the water column, neither sinking nor rising. This state of neutral buoyancy is essential for divers to conserve energy, minimize disturbance to the underwater environment, and enhance safety. Achieving neutral buoyancy allows you to move gracefully through the water and maintain a stable position, making it easier to observe marine life and navigate dive sites effectively.

- **Overweighting:** Overweighting is a common issue among divers. It occurs when divers carry an excessive amount of weight, either due to misjudgment, lack of experience, or uncertainty about buoyancy requirements. This can lead to several challenges underwater, including difficulty achieving neutral buoyancy, increased air consumption, and compromised comfort and safety.

Causes: Divers may overestimate the amount of weight needed to achieve neutral buoyancy, leading to an unnecessary burden. Novice divers may struggle to achieve neutral buoyancy and rely on excess weight to compensate for poor buoyancy control.

Consequences: Carrying excess weight requires more effort to maintain buoyancy, resulting in higher air consumption and shorter dive times. Excessive weight can make it challenging to ascend safely, potentially leading to rapid ascents and increased risk of decompression sickness. The additional weight can cause discomfort and fatigue, hindering movement and agility underwater.

Mitigation: Conduct a buoyancy check before each dive to determine the minimum amount of weight required for neutral buoyancy. Add or remove weight gradually based on buoyancy test results and dive conditions, rather than relying on guesswork. Improve buoyancy control skills through training and practice, focusing on fine-tuning trim and maintaining neutral buoyancy throughout the dive.

- **Underweighting**: Underweighting is the opposite of overweighting, where divers carry too little weight to achieve neutral buoyancy. While less common than overweighting, underweighting can still pose significant challenges underwater, affecting buoyancy control, stability, and safety.

Causes: Divers may underestimate the amount of weight needed to achieve neutral buoyancy, especially in situations where additional weight is necessary, such as wearing thicker wetsuits or using aluminum tanks. Some divers fear sinking and opt for minimal weight, even if it compromises buoyancy control and stability underwater.

Consequences: Underweighting can cause divers to float uncontrollably or struggle to maintain depth, resulting in inefficient propulsion and navigation. Insufficient weight can lead to instability and erratic movements underwater, increasing the risk of collisions with the environment or other divers. Constant adjustments to maintain buoyancy can lead to increased air consumption and shorter dive times.

Mitigation: Conduct a thorough buoyancy check before each dive to determine the optimal amount of weight required for neutral buoyancy. Consider factors such as exposure suit thickness, tank type, and dive conditions when determining weight requirements and make adjustments accordingly. Practice buoyancy control drills and exercises in controlled environments to improve skill proficiency and confidence in managing buoyancy underwater.

- **Difficulty Maintaining Trim**: Maintaining proper trim, or horizontal body position, is crucial for achieving efficient propulsion, minimizing drag, and conserving energy during dives. However, many divers struggle to maintain optimal trim, leading to inefficient swimming and increased air consumption.

Causes: Incorrect weight distribution or excessive weight on certain body parts can cause divers to adopt a head-down or feet-up orientation, disrupting trim. Lack of awareness or control over body position can cause divers to drift out of trim, especially in strong currents or turbulent conditions. Inefficient finning techniques can contribute to poor trim and stability underwater.

Consequences: Improper trim increases drag and resistance, requiring more effort to move through the water and leading to higher air consumption. Suboptimal trim negatively impacts propulsion and maneuverability, making it harder to navigate effectively and conserve energy during dives. Divers in poor trim are more likely to come into contact with the environment or other equipment, increasing the risk of entanglement or damage to marine life.

Mitigation: Ensure weight is evenly distributed throughout the body to maintain a horizontal trim position and avoid imbalance. Develop awareness of body position and alignment underwater, focusing on maintaining a streamlined posture and minimizing unnecessary movements. Practice efficient finning techniques, such as the flutter kick or modified frog kick, to achieve smooth propulsion and maintain trim. Adjust equipment configuration, such as tank positioning and harness setup, to optimize trim and reduce drag during dives. Incorporate trim drills and exercises into dive training and practice sessions to improve body control and trim awareness underwater.

Responding to Equipment Malfunctions

Scuba diving is a rewarding and exhilarating activity, but it also comes with its fair share of challenges. Diving with malfunctioning gear or experiencing buoyancy problems can quickly turn a calm dive into a stressful situation.

This chapter is dedicated to helping you understand and overcome some of the common obstacles that divers may face in their underwater adventures.

Let's explore common equipment challenges and how to mitigate them through proper maintenance and familiarity.

Gear Malfunctions

Diving equipment is your lifeline underwater, but like any mechanical device, it can encounter malfunctions. Understanding common gear issues and knowing how to address them is essential for every diver.

- **Regulator Free-Flow**: Imagine this scenario - you're underwater, enjoying the beauty of the reef, when suddenly your regulator starts delivering air uncontrollably, blasting bubbles out of your mouthpiece. This is a regulator free-flow, a situation every diver hopes to avoid but should be prepared to handle.

Causes:

- First-stage failure: A malfunction in the first stage of the regulator can lead to uncontrolled airflow.
- Second-stage malfunction: Issues with the second-stage regulator, such as a stuck valve or damaged diaphragm, can result in a free-flow.
- Freezing: Extremely cold water temperatures can cause ice to form inside the regulator, leading to a free-flow.

Mitigation:

1. Perform regular equipment maintenance: Ensure your regulator is serviced and inspected by a certified technician according to manufacturer guidelines.
2. Carry a properly functioning alternate air source (octopus) in case of a free-flow.
3. Practice proper breathing techniques to reduce the risk of triggering a free-flow.
4. Monitor your air supply and dive depth to avoid exceeding safe limits.
5. Stay calm and controlled if a free-flow occurs, signal your dive buddy, and ascend safely if necessary.

- **Leaking Masks:** Another common gear issue divers may encounter is a leaking mask. A leaking mask can cause discomfort and impair vision, making it essential to address promptly.

Causes:

- Poor fit: A mask that does not seal properly to your face can allow water to seep in.
- Hair or debris: Hair or debris trapped between the mask skirt and your face can create gaps, allowing water to enter.
- Mask damage: Tears or holes in the mask skirt can compromise its ability to create a watertight seal.

Mitigation:

1. Ensure your mask fits properly and forms a seal without gaps.
2. Use mask defogging solution to prevent fogging, which can exacerbate leaks.
3. Clear any hair or debris from the mask skirt before donning it.
4. If a leak occurs during the dive, perform a mask clearance by pressing the top of the mask and exhaling through your nose to expel water.
5. Consider carrying a spare mask as a backup in case of persistent leaks.

- **Failing Buoyancy Compensator Device (BCD):** A malfunctioning buoyancy compensator device (BCD) can compromise a diver's ability to control buoyancy, ascent, and descent, posing a significant safety risk underwater.

Causes:

- Inflator malfunction: Issues with the inflator mechanism, such as sticking buttons or damaged O-rings, can prevent proper inflation or deflation of the BCD.
- Bladder puncture: Tears or punctures in the BCD bladder can cause air leakage, leading to buoyancy issues.
- Overpressurization: Accidental overinflation of the BCD bladder, either manually or due to equipment malfunction, can cause uncontrolled ascent or buoyancy fluctuations.

Mitigation:

1. Conduct a pre-dive inspection of the BCD, checking for signs of wear, damage, or malfunction in the inflator mechanism, bladder, and valves.
2. Test the inflator button and oral/power inflator for proper function before entering the water.
3. Practice emergency BCD inflation and deflation procedures, including manual inflation using the oral/power inflator and rapid deflation using the dump valves.
4. Carry a spare BCD or alternate buoyancy device as a backup in case of BCD failure during the dive.
5. Stay vigilant and monitor buoyancy control throughout the dive, making adjustments as needed to maintain proper trim and stability.

.

- **Malfunctioning Dive Computers:** Dive computers are valuable tools for monitoring depth, bottom time, and decompression limits during dives. However, they can malfunction, leading to inaccurate readings or complete failure.

Causes:

- Battery issues: Low battery levels or battery failure can cause the dive computer to malfunction.
- Water damage: Exposure to water or moisture can damage the internal components of the dive computer, leading to malfunctions
- Impact damage: Dropping the dive computer can cause internal damage and malfunctions.

Mitigation:

1. Replace the battery according to manufacturer recommendations or before each dive trip.
2. Rinse the dive computer with fresh water after each dive to remove salt and debris, and store it in a protective case when not in use.
3. Avoid exposing the dive computer to extreme temperatures, direct sunlight, or impact.
4. Carry a backup timing device, such as a dive watch or bottom timer, in case of dive computer failure.

Dealing with Underwater Pressure

Understanding How Pressure Acts on the Body

As scuba divers descend into the depths of the ocean, we enter a world where the laws of physics govern our every move. One of the most significant forces we encounter is pressure – the relentless force exerted by the water column above us.

At the surface, we experience atmospheric pressure, the weight of the air pressing down on our bodies. As we descend underwater, this pressure increases rapidly with depth. Every 33 feet (10 meters) of descent adds approximately 1 atmosphere (ATM) of pressure, causing significant physiological changes.

The most noticeable effect of pressure is on air-containing spaces within the body, such as the ears, sinuses, and lungs. As pressure increases, these air spaces compress, as we have already seen in the chapter of Equalization.

Additionally, pressure affects the density of the gases we breathe, leading to increased gas consumption rates with depth. The deeper we go, the more this air is compressed, we must therefore monitor our air supply carefully and maintain a steady breathing rhythm to conserve air and avoid running out of gas during the dive.

As seen previously, pressure also plays a crucial role in decompression, the process of safely ascending to the surface and off-gassing excess nitrogen absorbed during the dive.

By understanding how pressure acts on the body is we can deal with it's reactions and navigate the underwater environment safely.

CHAPTER 9:

Safety and Emergency Procedures

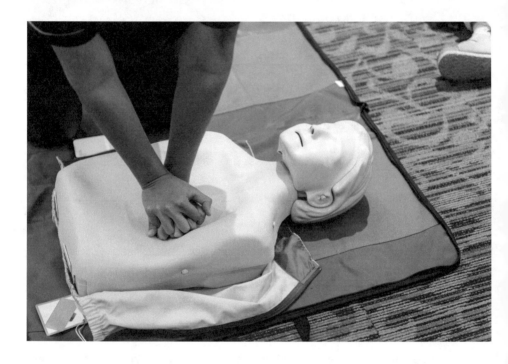

As you progress through your diving journey, it's crucial to be prepared for **unexpected situations** and equipped with the **knowledge and skills** to respond effectively to **emergencies**. Throughout this chapter, we will delve in **first aid** for divers, communication and the buddy system, and handling emergency ascents.

By mastering these essential safety measures, you will gain the **confidence** and **competence** to navigate potential challenges and **respond calmly** to **emergencies underwater**.

First Aid for Divers

As you progress through your diving journey, being equipped with the knowledge and skills to handle common diving injuries and emergencies is paramount for ensuring safety and well-being underwater.

- **Managing Diving Injuries**: Learn how to effectively treat cuts, scrapes, puncture wounds, and other injuries commonly encountered during diving activities. You will discuss proper wound care techniques using the resources available in your dive kit, including bandages, antiseptics, and wound dressings.

- **Oxygen Administration**: Discover the importance of oxygen therapy in treating diving-related emergencies, such as decompression sickness (DCS) or respiratory distress. You will learn how to assemble and use emergency oxygen equipment provided in your dive kit, administer oxygen safely, and monitor the patient's condition for signs of improvement or deterioration.

- **Recognizing Diving Illnesses**: Familiarize yourself with the signs and symptoms of diving-related illnesses, including nitrogen narcosis and barotrauma. Discover the importance of prompt recognition and intervention to prevent further complications and ensure the safety of yourself and your dive buddy.

- **Cardiopulmonary Resuscitation (CPR) and Rescue Breathing**: Master the life-saving skills of CPR and rescue breathing, essential techniques for responding to cardiac arrest or drowning incidents underwater. Learn how to perform chest compressions, deliver rescue breaths, and coordinate CPR efforts with your dive buddy or dive team leader.

- **Utilizing First Aid Equipment**: Explore the contents and use of first aid kits provided by your dive center or dive boat. Learn how to identify and utilize essential first aid supplies, including bandages, antiseptics, airway adjuncts, and oxygen delivery devices, in emergency situations.

Communication and Buddy System

Clear communication and close cooperation with your dive buddy are essential components of safe diving practices, enabling you to navigate the underwater environment and **respond effectively to emergencies.**

- **Underwater Communication Technique**s: Underwater communication is essential for coordinating with your dive buddy and ensuring a safe dive. The primary methods of communication underwater include hand signals and dive slate messages. We will explore standardized hand signals for essential messages such as "OK," "out of air," "ascend," and "descend." These signals are universally recognized and help divers convey critical information quickly and clearly. Additionally, in conditions where visibility is low or hand signals are insufficient, dive slates can be used to write messages. Mastering these communication techniques will enhance your ability to stay connected and respond effectively in various underwater scenarios.

- **Pre-Dive Communication Plans**: Establishing pre-dive communication plans with your dive buddy is crucial for ensuring mutual understanding and preparedness for emergencies. Before entering the water, discuss dive objectives, emergency procedures, and communication signals. This pre-dive briefing helps set clear expectations and fosters a sense of confidence and trust between dive buddies. By thoroughly reviewing each other's equipment, confirming dive plans, and agreeing on signals, you create a foundation for effective communication and coordination throughout the dive. This proactive approach minimizes misunderstandings and enhances safety.

- **Maintaining Visual Contact and Proximity**: Maintaining visual contact and proximity with your dive buddy is essential for immediate assistance and effective communication. Staying close to your buddy throughout the dive ensures that you can quickly signal for help or offer assistance in case of an emergency. Techniques for staying close include proper positioning, such as swimming side by side or slightly behind your buddy, and using effective signaling methods to maintain awareness of each other's presence. Practicing these techniques helps prevent separation, reduces anxiety, and ensures that both divers can enjoy a safer and more relaxed dive experience.

- **Buddy Checks and Communication Drills**: Implementing regular buddy checks and communication drills reinforces safety protocols and readiness for emergencies. Pre-dive buddy checks involve inspecting each other's equipment to ensure everything is functioning correctly. This step includes verifying that masks, fins, regulators, and other gear are secure and operational. Reviewing emergency procedures and practicing communication signals with your dive buddy are equally important. These drills help you and your buddy stay familiar with each other's equipment and reinforce the signals you'll use underwater. Regular practice of these routines ensures seamless coordination and teamwork, enhancing your ability to respond effectively to any situation that may arise during the dive.

By mastering underwater communication techniques, establishing thorough pre-dive communication plans, maintaining visual contact and proximity, and conducting regular buddy checks and communication drills, you and your dive buddy will be better prepared to handle the challenges of scuba diving. These practices not only enhance safety but also contribute to a more enjoyable and confident diving experience.

Dive Health and Fitness

It's important to recognize the significant role that **physical health** and fitness play in ensuring your safety and well-being underwater. From managing equalization challenges to dealing with common health concerns like seasickness, being in good physical condition can enhance your diving performance and safety.

Let's view some key things you can do to stay in the best shape.

- **Physical Conditioning**: Maintaining good physical health is paramount for safe and enjoyable diving experiences. Divers should prioritize fitness to enhance endurance, strength, and flexibility, which are essential for managing the demands of diving. Regular cardiovascular exercises, strength training, and flexibility exercises can improve overall fitness levels and help prevent injuries. Additionally, managing equalization challenges, such as ear or sinus issues, is crucial for comfortable and safe diving. Techniques like equalization maneuvers and proper descent techniques can help divers manage pressure changes effectively.

- **Dive Fitness**: Dive fitness assessments are valuable tools for evaluating an individual's readiness for diving, particularly for older divers or those with pre-existing health conditions. Regular check-ups with healthcare professionals, including physicians and dive medicine specialists, can help identify any medical concerns that may affect diving safety. It's essential to address any health issues proactively and follow medical advice to ensure safe participation in diving activities.

- **Skill Refinement**: Continuous skill development is key to becoming a proficient and confident diver. Divers should regularly practice and refine essential skills, such as buoyancy control, navigation, and communication, to improve their competence underwater. Participating in specialty courses or workshops focused on specific diving skills can provide valuable opportunities for skill enhancement. Additionally, divers should seek feedback from instructors or experienced dive buddies to identify areas for improvement and work towards mastery of essential diving techniques.

- **Confidence-Building**: Building confidence underwater is a gradual process that requires practice, experience, and self-assurance. Divers can boost their confidence by investing in additional training opportunities, such as advanced courses or specialty certifications, to expand their knowledge and skills. Repeated dives in varying conditions help divers become more familiar with different environments and build trust in their abilities. Seeking guidance and mentorship from experienced divers or instructors can also provide valuable support and encouragement for building confidence in challenging diving situations. Ultimately, cultivating a positive mindset and believing in one's capabilities are essential for developing confidence as a diver.

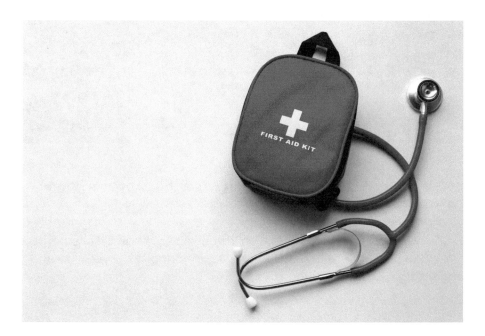

CHAPTER 10:

Final Assessments and Certification

Congratulations on reaching Chapter 10 of the **PADI Open Water Diver** Course!

In this chapter, we will guide you through the final assessments and certification process, marking the culmination of your journey to **becoming a certified diver.**

Written Exams and Practical Assessments

At the end of your course you will face written exams and practical assessments to evaluate your understanding and proficiency in scuba diving. These assessments are designed to test your theoretical knowledge and practical skills acquired throughout the course.

Written Exams: Prepare for written exams by reviewing course materials, textbooks, and any supplementary resources provided by your instructor. Exams typically cover topics such as dive theory, dive planning, safety procedures, and environmental awareness. Take your time to read each question carefully and ensure that you understand the concepts before providing your answers. Written exams are typically conducted in a controlled environment, either online or in-person. Be sure to pay close attention to key concepts and terminology. Practice answering sample questions to familiarize yourself with the format and style of the exam.

Practical Assessments: Practical assessments involve demonstrating your diving skills in real or simulated underwater scenarios. These assessments may take place in confined water environments, such as swimming pools, or open water settings, depending on your course structure. Tasks may include equipment setup and checks, buoyancy control, underwater navigation, mask clearing, regulator recovery, emergency ascents, and buddy assistance techniques. Practice these skills with your instructor or dive buddy, focusing on precision, efficiency, and safety. Seek feedback from your instructor to identify areas for improvement and refine your techniques accordingly.

Reviewing Your Performance

Take time to review your answers and assess your performance objectively. Identify areas where you excelled and areas where you may need further practice or improvement.

Seek Feedback: Don't hesitate to seek feedback from your instructor or dive buddies. They can provide valuable insights into your performance and offer constructive criticism to help you enhance your skills. Use this feedback as a learning opportunity to refine your techniques and become a better diver.

Continuous Learning: Remember that learning doesn't stop with certification. Embrace a mindset of continuous improvement and lifelong learning in your diving journey. Take advantage of advanced courses, workshops, and dive experiences to expand your knowledge and skills further. Stay updated on industry trends, safety protocols, and environmental conservation efforts to remain a knowledgeable and responsible diver.

Receiving Your PADI Open Water Certification

Your **certification** signifies that you have met the standards set by PADI for safe and competent recreational diving.

Celebrating Your Achievement: Celebrate your certification with pride and joy! You've worked hard to reach this milestone, and it's a testament to your dedication and perseverance. Share your achievement with friends and family, and relish in the excitement of becoming a certified diver.

Responsibilities as a Certified Diver: With certification comes responsibilities. As a certified diver, you are entrusted with the safety of yourself and your fellow divers. Adhere to safe diving practices, respect the underwater environment, and uphold the principles of dive conservation. Remember that with great freedom comes great responsibility, and strive to be a conscientious and responsible diver at all times.

CHAPTER 11:
Continuing Your Dive Journey

Embarking on the path of scuba diving is just the beginning of a **lifelong adventure.**

Consider exploring the **next steps** and **opportunities** for you to enhance your skills, pursue advanced certifications, and deepen your connection with the underwater world.

Advanced Training and Specialties

Congratulations on completing your PADI Open Water Diver course!

Now that you've mastered the basics of scuba diving, it's time to take the next step and pursue advanced certifications. In this section, we'll explore the benefits of advancing your diving skills and knowledge through courses like the PADI Advanced Open Water Diver certification.

Advanced Open Water Diver Certification

Advancing to the Advanced Open Water Diver certification opens up a world of possibilities in the underwater realm. This course builds upon the foundational skills learned in the Open Water Diver course and expands your diving horizons. By completing advanced certifications, you'll deepen your knowledge, refine your skills, and increase your confidence as a diver. Whether you're interested in exploring deeper dive sites, navigating complex underwater environments, or diving at night, the Advanced Open Water Diver course offers a pathway to new and exciting diving adventures.

In the Advanced Open Water Diver course, you'll have the opportunity to develop specialized diving skills and experiences. From mastering underwater navigation techniques to exploring deeper dive sites, night diving, and wreck diving, each specialty dive opens up new possibilities for exploration and adventure. These skills not only enhance your diving abilities but also allow you to access a wider range of dive sites and environments with confidence and competence.

Specialty Diver Courses

Specialty diver courses provide divers with the opportunity to explore specific areas of interest within the realm of scuba diving. Whether you're passionate about underwater photography, marine biology, wreck exploration, or drift diving, there's a specialty course to suit your interests. These courses allow you to tailor your diving experiences to your passions and gain specialized knowledge and skills in your chosen area of focus.

Becoming a Rescue Diver

Becoming a Rescue Diver is an essential step in advancing your diving skills and ensuring the safety of yourself and your fellow divers. This certification equips you with the knowledge and skills to handle dive emergencies and assist others in need. As a Rescue Diver, you'll learn how to recognize and respond to various underwater emergencies, including diver distress, equipment malfunctions, and underwater accidents.

Rescue Diver training involves realistic scenario-based exercises that simulate emergency situations encountered in diving. Through hands-on training and simulated rescue scenarios, you'll learn how to assess and manage dive emergencies effectively, provide assistance to distressed divers, and coordinate emergency responses with dive buddies and professional rescuers. By mastering these critical skills, you'll be prepared to handle emergency situations with confidence and competence, making you a valuable asset to any diving team.

Professional Diving

For those seeking to take their diving to the next level, the path to becoming a Divemaster or Scuba Instructor offers a rewarding and fulfilling career in the diving industry. As a Divemaster or Instructor, you'll have the opportunity to share your passion for diving with others, lead dive excursions, and inspire new divers to explore the wonders of the underwater world. These roles come with responsibilities, including guiding dives, assisting instructors with courses, and ensuring the safety and enjoyment of divers under your supervision.

Joining the Dive Community

Joining the diving community is an exciting step that opens up a world of camaraderie, shared experiences, and lifelong friendships. Whether you're a newly certified diver or a seasoned underwater enthusiast, becoming part of the diving community offers numerous benefits and opportunities for growth.

- **Local Dive Clubs:** One of the best ways to connect with fellow divers in your area is by joining a local dive club or association. These clubs often host regular meetings, social events, and dive outings, providing opportunities to meet and dive with like-minded individuals. Joining a dive club allows you to share dive stories, exchange tips and advice, and organize group dives to explore new dive sites together.

- **Online Forums and Social Media:** In today's digital age, online forums and social media platforms provide a virtual space for divers to connect, share experiences, and seek advice from the diving community worldwide. Joining online diving forums, Facebook groups, or Instagram communities allows you to interact with divers from diverse backgrounds and locations, share dive photos and videos, and stay updated on the latest diving news and trends.

- **Dive Shops and Resorts:** Dive shops and resorts are hubs of activity for divers, offering a range of services, from equipment sales and rentals to dive training and guided dive trips. By frequenting your local dive shop or visiting dive resorts during your travels, you'll have the opportunity to meet fellow divers, participate in dive events and workshops, and join organized dive excursions to nearby dive sites.

- **Volunteer Opportunities:** Many dive organizations and conservation groups offer volunteer opportunities for divers interested in giving back to the underwater world. Whether it's participating in beach cleanups, coral reef restoration projects, or marine life monitoring initiatives, volunteering allows you to contribute to marine conservation efforts while connecting with other passionate divers who share your commitment to protecting the oceans.

- **Dive Expos and Events:** Dive expos, trade shows, and events are excellent platforms for divers to come together, learn from industry experts, and explore the latest diving gear and technologies. Attending dive expos allows you to network with fellow divers, attend informative seminars and workshops, and discover new dive destinations and experiences to add to your bucket list.

- **Dive Travel:** Traveling to dive destinations around the world is a fantastic way to immerse yourself in the global diving community and experience diverse underwater ecosystems. Whether you're exploring tropical coral reefs, diving with sharks in the open ocean, or exploring historical wrecks, dive travel offers endless opportunities to connect with fellow divers, share unforgettable experiences, and create lasting memories together.

Exploring Diving Destinations

- **Embark on Global Adventures:** Dive travel offers divers the opportunity to explore some of the most breathtaking underwater landscapes on the planet. Whether you're drawn to the crystal-clear waters of tropical destinations like the Maldives or Fiji, the rich biodiversity of marine sanctuaries like the Galápagos Islands or Raja Ampat, or the adrenaline-pumping drift dives of destinations like the Red Sea or Indonesia, the world is your oyster when it comes to dive travel. Delve into the excitement of discovering new dive sites, encountering unique marine species, and immersing yourself in different cultures and environments while on dive trips abroad.

- **Planning Your Dive Trips:** Planning a dive trip requires careful consideration of factors such as destination, seasonality, dive conditions, and logistics. Research and select dive destinations, book accommodations and dive operators, and prepare for the unique challenges and opportunities of diving in foreign waters. From packing essential dive gear to obtaining necessary travel documents and insurance coverage, proper planning ensures smooth and enjoyable dive travel experiences.

- **Conservation and Preservation:** As stewards of the ocean, it's essential for divers to prioritize conservation and preservation efforts while traveling. Pay special importance to respecting local regulations, minimizing your impact on delicate marine ecosystems, and supporting local conservation initiatives aimed at protecting marine biodiversity and habitats. From practicing responsible dive behavior to participating in eco-friendly dive tours and beach cleanups, every diver has a role to play in preserving the underwater world for future generations to enjoy.

CHAPTER 12:

Tips for Responsible Diving

Responsible diving is crucial for the **preservation** of our underwater ecosystems and the **safety** of all divers.

This chapter will provide essential tips on marine conservation, minimizing your ecological footprint, and becoming a conscious diver.

Marine Conservation and Respect for Nature

Responsible Diving Practices for Environmental Conservation

Scuba diving provides us with an incredible opportunity to explore and connect with the underwater world. With this privilege comes a responsibility to protect and preserve the delicate ecosystems we encounter beneath the waves.

Marine Conservation Awareness: Educate yourself about marine conservation issues and the importance of preserving underwater ecosystems. Stay informed about local marine protected areas, endangered species, and conservation initiatives in the areas where you dive. Understanding the challenges facing our oceans helps you become a more informed and responsible diver.

Respect for Marine Life: Treat marine life with respect and admiration, observing from a distance and avoiding any interactions that could harm or disturb aquatic creatures. Refrain from touching, feeding, or chasing marine animals, and never remove souvenirs or specimens from their natural habitat. This helps maintain the natural behavior and health of marine species and ensures that future divers can enjoy the same vibrant underwater experiences.

Respect the Ecosystem: Be mindful of your impact on the underwater environment. Practice good buoyancy control to avoid accidentally damaging coral reefs or stirring up sediment that can smother marine life. Use reef-safe sunscreen to prevent chemical damage to coral ecosystems. By taking these simple steps, you contribute to the preservation of delicate underwater habitats and promote a healthy marine ecosystem.

Minimizing Your Ecological Footprint

By adopting sustainable practices both in and out of the water, we can help preserve marine environments for future generations.

- **Sustainable Dive Practices:** One of the most direct ways to reduce your ecological footprint is by practicing sustainable diving. This begins with mastering buoyancy control to avoid accidental contact with the reef. Poor buoyancy can lead to kicking up sediment, which can smother coral and disrupt marine life. Additionally, divers should always be aware of their body and equipment, ensuring they do not touch or damage underwater structures. Using a reef hook in strong currents can prevent you from drifting into sensitive areas.

- **Reducing Plastic Use:** Plastic pollution is one of the most pressing environmental issues affecting our oceans. Divers can help combat this by reducing their use of single-use plastics. Bring a reusable water bottle, shopping bag, and straw on your dive trips. Choose dive operators that prioritize sustainability and avoid using plastic bags for your equipment. Participating in beach and underwater cleanups also directly addresses the problem, helping to remove plastic debris from marine environments.

- **Supporting Marine Conservation:** Supporting marine conservation organizations and initiatives is a powerful way to make a difference. These groups work tirelessly to protect marine ecosystems through research, advocacy, and on-the-ground conservation efforts. Donations, volunteer work, or simply spreading awareness about their causes can significantly amplify their impact. Many dive operators collaborate with conservation groups, offering opportunities to engage in citizen science projects or coral restoration activities.

- **Educating Others:** Sharing your knowledge and passion for marine conservation can inspire others to take action. Whether it's through social media, community presentations, or informal conversations, educating others about the importance of protecting our oceans helps build a broader coalition of environmentally conscious divers.

Being a Conscious Diver

- **Environmental Awareness:** Engaging with the local diving community and participating in conservation initiatives are excellent ways to make a positive impact. Join local dive groups that organize regular beach cleanups or underwater debris removal dives. Collaborate with fellow divers to advocate for marine protection and lobby for stronger environmental regulations. Raising awareness about the importance of preserving marine ecosystems can also be achieved through community outreach programs, educational workshops, and social media campaigns. By working together, divers can create a collective voice that supports marine conservation efforts and promotes sustainable diving practices.

- **Community Engagement**: Engaging with the local diving community and participating in conservation initiatives are excellent ways to make a positive impact. Join local dive groups that organize regular beach cleanups or underwater debris removal dives. Collaborate with fellow divers to advocate for marine protection and lobby for stronger environmental regulations. Raising awareness about the importance of preserving marine ecosystems can also be achieved through community outreach programs, educational workshops, and social media campaigns. By working together, divers can create a collective voice that supports marine conservation efforts and promotes sustainable diving practices.

By embracing these tips for responsible diving, you can contribute to the conservation and protection of our precious underwater world for generations to come. As divers, we have a unique opportunity to be ambassadors for the ocean, promoting awareness, respect, and stewardship wherever our underwater adventures take us.

LOGBOOKS
Personal Diving Logbook

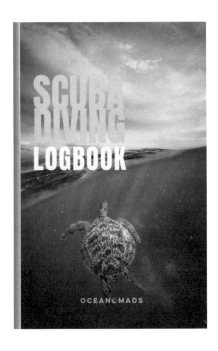  

Utilising a personal **diving logbook** is an excellent way to keep a record of your scuba diving experiences.

It not only helps you reminisce about your underwater adventures but also serves as a **valuable tool** for tracking your progress, dive history, and safety information.

We have created our very own **Scuba Divers Logbook** for you to keep up-to-date with your latest diving adventures.

It includes all the relevant information you need and contains all the pages necessary to keep track of your next **120 dives**!

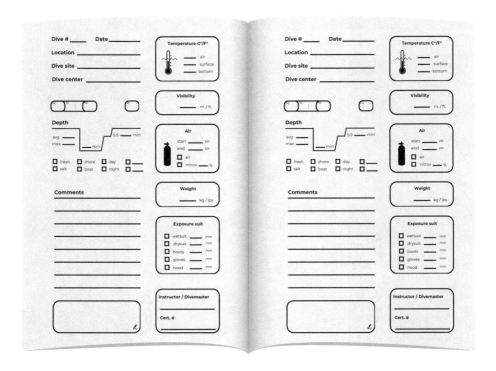

You can find our Logbook on **Amazon** and have it delivered in no time, ready for your next diving adventures!

Don't miss the opportunity, head on over and order your copy now!

Made in United States
Troutdale, OR
09/05/2024

22617244R00051